THE GHOST OF
ANTHONY KE

To James,
It's great
to have you at Edge
Hill.

SWAN PRESS
DUBLIN

First Published by the Swan Press 2014
32 Joy Street
Ringsend
Dublin 4
Republic of Ireland

ISBN 978-0-95604-968-1

Acknowledgments

A number of these poems have been previously published in,
journals, magazines, newspapers, anthologies and websites.
Including: Rialto, Poetry Ireland Review, Black Mountain Review,
The SHOp, Stinging Fly, HQ, The Sunday Tribune, The Edgeworth
Papers, Magicwrite, the Irish Independent, Female First Magazine,
The Judas Goat, Post -Poetry Magazine/The Internationalist, Prose
on a Bed of Rhyme, Mallow Star, Bridgewater Hall, The Delinquent.

The author would like to thank those who gave generously of their
advice and encouragement including: Austin Wilde, Robert
Sheppard, Cath Cole, Maureen Airey, Sheila Jones, Ailsa Cox, Dan
Pantano, Steven Maxwell, Jonny Clarke, Dawn Wild, Mary
Guckian. James Conway, Emma Stewart, Ellen Rivas-Torrecillas
and Sue Burns

Dedication
To my two original mentors, Alan Marsden and Frank Pearce; and
those who gifted me their love and unconditional regard: My darling
wife, Paula Keating, my mother, Mary Keating, Eski, Jacquie Eckett,
and to my very special and much missed sister of mercy, Kate
Llewellyn Holland (RIP).

CONTENTS

ORIGIN AND ASH

A KIND OF LOVING

CAMINO

LOST AND FOUND

ORIGIN AND ASH

SOMETHING FOR THE WEEKEND

It was an object of wonder to me,
Discreetly wrapped
In a folded handkerchief,
My father's knuckle-duster,
Sunday to Thursday
Tucked away in a chest of drawers,
Beneath underpants and socks.

An off the shelf leveller
Of the public bar class,
Four raised ridges
Embossed with a floral motif,
Slick as Vaselined hair,
Deliberate as pale blue eyes.

On Friday and Saturday nights
He tapped his jacket pocket,
Laughingly reassuring my mother
That he wasn't heading out, without his
"Something for the weekend".

REMEMBRANCE DAY

I knew them in my youth, old soldiers,
Senses so basted with horror
That sleep tortured them,
Regulars at libraries, benches and public bars,
Lonely men, that ate in hot plate cafes.

Too often forgotten and shunned,
Grateful to talk with an ardent boy,
They spoke of gas and Whizz-Bangs,
Comrades and waste,
Testifying against eternal youth
Having eaten bully beef amongst its fetid decay.

And now the last of them is in the barracks of the dead
We fawn on their memory, having ignored their lives,
The odd, the lonely, disfigured and mad,
Regiments that marched from bedsits to pauper's graves,
Without wreaths, flags or tears.

2 TO 1

Furtively through the side door
Always a little ashamed
Cars and buses streaming past on Highgate Road
Where the brash shop front gleamed with gold
Sovereigns, crucifixes, watches, engagement rings
The light of long dead stars reaching acquisitive eyes
A testament to the lining in every cloud
In ticka ticka Timex times

It need not glitter to be gold
But it helped
A good suit, an iron, or a wedding band

Deal done
A pound or thirty bob
Interest and the redemption date
Scratched on a blue card ticket
Written in triplicate
Three pens, three inkpots
One hand working the symmetry

Food on the table for another couple of days
She wore a washer on her wedding finger
Hoping he wouldn't lose his wages
Before she could get them back
And that she wouldn't have to face his rage
When he found out about his Sunday best

THE JUNCTION TAVERN

Embossed, tobacco stained
Magnolia paper
Peeling off the walls.
Red cracked lino,
Scattered tables with bentwood chairs,
Newspapers, betting slips and pencil stubs.

A conspiracy of Caribbeans and Celts
Playing dominoes and cards
In an edgy stillness.
The silence and muttered words
Occasionally rocked by shouts,
Bricks slammed on tables,
A flurry of abuse
For misplayed trumps or dots,
Choreographed aggression
And occasionally a fist,
Until stillness settled once again
To the sucking of teeth and clearing of phlegm.

Out there the '60s was happening
In the Junction nothing changed.
They re-emerge in my memory
Through a fog of smoke, beer and piss.
Scully, O'Gorman, O' Driscoll,
Jamaican George and Welsh John
In their collars and ties.
On Sunday morning their Sunday best:
For protocol had to be observed
To honour the utilitarian pleasures of the working man.

RICH MAN, POOR MAN, BEGGAR MAN, THIEF

I remember
My father the tin master
Shaping bottle crowns
To fit the electric slot
And the thin sound of his forgery
As they hit the plundered steel box

But most of all
I remember my mother's excuses
To the man from the Electricity Board
Who benignly listened
As he passed her the bottle tops
In exchange for coins

And the electric man's good natured grin
As he fixed yet another brass padlock
That would not be there on his return

WERNICKE-KORSAKOFF SYNDROME

I read of a parasitoid wasp
That injects its eggs into a caterpillar
Along with a virus of forgetfulness
That causes it, in time, to destroy itself.
The caterpillar, now a living larder,
Pulses its blood to the maggots
That when ready to pupate
Incise and burst
Through the caterpillar's skin,
Triggering the crazed surrogate
To wrap the wasp's young
In the silk cocoon
It forgot to weave for itself,
And to guard them with a parent's rage
Until dying of starvation,
Its hollowed body
Having become
A sarcophagus of the self.

THE GOOD WIFE

I watch my mother's daily labour
In the gulag of her marriage
Toileting, shaving, and above all
Getting his parting straight
An office that is a matter of homage to her
Though it has lost all meaning to him

PORTRAIT

I now rarely look on you as a man
Or as my father
But more as an object

As the remembering of who you still are
Invokes in me the churning fear
That must have been felt by Dorian Gray
In the presence of his corrupted self

AN INSTITUTIONAL BIRTH, 1947

In the moments after she gave birth
She reached for language
Determined to question the absence
She felt even more keenly
Than the one on her left hand

But before harnessing its possibilities
A voice redolent with faith
Offered the judgment:

"It's just as well,
the child had a head like a rockery"

Turning into her grief
She swaddled that absence in silence
In the milk heavy weeks
And through the absence laden years
She wondered and wondered
Was 'the child' a boy or a girl

EVE GOES DANCING, 1948

She returned home after her time away,
An open secret branding her with sinful blood,
For weeks she haunted the asylum of pretence
Sheltering from spiteful tongues,
Grieving that absence without a name.
But now her figure back,
Knowing that things must seem as before
She headed to the dance.

In the hall she found a space in unfamiliar shadows,
A space that grew and grew as she rooted in reality,
A wall flower, sketched in hand over mouth conversations,
Despised and thrilling in equal measure.
Too pretty, too dangerous to be seen with or to ignore,
Acknowledged, when they had to,
By those who used to call her friend,
Their tepid smiles distillations of pity and distain.

And when the last dance was done
Expectant boys gathered like crows,
Emboldened by porter
And the thinning shame of departures,
They moved in,
Hoping for a taste of the forbidden fruit,
They imagined she clutched
As she fell from respectability.

Understanding her commodity she longed for home
And her parents benign disappointment,
Just as the boys longed for darkened corners
Away from their mammy's contorting shame.
Rejecting their advances she walked home,
A woman in the dignity of silence,
The air pulsing with the scornful boy's rebuke,
'Whore'.

NO RETURN

Her bag packed
one last look
before turning her back
her farewells received
with relief and regret

She had left before
left to return
from kin to faith to kin again
but this time she journeyed to a foreign shore

She knew as they did
that Lilith once kissed
could not remain in the garden
tainted as she was
beyond a man's command

On her way to the square
passing Murphy's store
she saw the old bitch
her mouth like a dog's arse
tight with piety
and she pitied the poor girl
that took her place
forced to wash the sanitary cloths of the Mrs
for a shop girl's wage

Getting off the bus in Cork
thinking she would be alone
she shoaled with exiles
krill in the mouth of a whale
anonymous and meaningless
their stories lost in the crowd

Keeping her appointment
on Maylor Street
she was examined like a horse
her teeth, withers and character
probed by the broker
to ensure she passed muster
for a domestic's life

Traded without spit on the hand
or a shilling for luck
she boarded the boat train to London
to be met at Euston
by a man of the respectable class
for whom it was planned
she would cook and clean

A doctor or a barrister perhaps
whose wife would be kinder to her than her own
or perhaps not
either way the ticket
this time was one way

A KIND OF LOVING

OFFERING

I will swim with you
In Vathi Fjord
And as you lay there drying
I will lick the salt from your skin

Weeping as it coats my tongue
I will tell you some lies
That you will not believe
And some others that you will

I will tell you of the dead relatives
That I keep in the loft
And of how my family wore purple
When purple really meant something around here

I will kneel in front of you
Head bowed and shaved
Holding a mirror fashioned from foam
Lacquered with a single drop of blood

As that most perfect of offerings

STILL LIFE

Yours is the beauty
Of distant voices
Conversations in a happy room
Unsullied by space and time

I can still taste the kafes glykys
You brought me in bed
Its bitter sweet
Sipped
As I traced the wheat of your hair
The fall of your back

For me you are still there
Framed in that window
Constant
Motionless against a blue sky

Sculpted in the moment
Punctuated by the harbour's din
That I felt the stillness
Of your decision to leave

The ferry to Piraeus
Churning your homeward sea

CINEMA OF THE SENSES

I remember Karen
From Whalley Range
I went to see Diva with her
At a cinema near Notting Hill
In 1982

I remember the darkness
Her blond hair, bright eyes
Perfume and the Aria from La Wally
And above all my desire
To reach out and touch her

I remember the journey home
And that she wanted to work in animation
When she finished at Manchester Poly
That same journey that I fell a little in love
With Karen from Whalley Range

And every time I smell her perfume,
Or hear La Wally
My senses take me back to her
In that darkened cinema
Near Notting Hill in 1982

FUCK YOU

The willow of your sex.
Black bob.
Blood red
lips,
Vagrant,
Squandered.
A scream's aftermath
harnesses silence,
Pressed into service;
An admission
that something went wrong.
Rituals that expunge
the ache of remembering
a party dress
discarded on some bastard's
floor,
Your safe harbour
as I raged about whatever.
No quarter given. Nor
asked for.
Later we fell into bed
fucking the familiar.
No names no pack drill,
Glancing more than connecting,
Regrets still an abstract
in search of language
that could bleed purpose
into our tightly wound world.

THE PROMISE

And I will make a tent
Of your black black hair
And beneath its canopy
You will devour me
With your three faces
Your silk hands flaming
Like flowers in bloom
As candle bright leaves
Float off on dark rivers
Swollen to flooding by the full moon

After Marichiko.

TOUCH

In the morning after we made love
you were Man Ray's violin woman.
As I read the Braille of contentment
down your spine
I could barely find the energy for movement.

This is how it should be.

A ROOM OF OUR OWN

I weary of crisp white linen
Of secret assignations
In rooms peddling the myth of the new
I long to make love with you
Between sheets stained with our history
In a room heavy with prospects
And passion's domestic neglect

RENEWAL i.m Kate

It is your anniversary today,
As always a bitter January day.
On the field this morning
The first small clump of snowdrops.

Ah, we transit through this world
With all the significance of a flea,
Constantly deluded
In the conceit we are worth more.

The truth is we are not.
The difference is I miss you,
Beyond missing
But you will return:

Perhaps as a rock or a bird,
A Nobel laureate,
Or a stickleback,
Your stuff is out there.
Your essence will coalesce.

Perhaps by happy coincidence,
As a snowdrop in this field.
But then again, what are the odds?

STAY, TILL WAKING

It is winter,
Our room is dark and warm,
Your hair the black plumes of funeral horses,
A portent of vivid absence.

You turn and the paleness of your skin,
Invades that restless stupor,
Inhabited by grief.

Flickering into waking,
Your sleep drunk eyes,
Meet me with an uncertain regard,
That softens into a smile of recognition.

Reaching out to stroke my hair,
You expose the poverty of language,
In an act of inviolable love.

Becalmed by your tenderness,
I drift into sleeping,
The narcotic of forgetting filling our room,
As we entwine our sentience,

Deeper and deeper into a blessed dreaming.

CAMINO

POTHIA

From here
Through the smoke and Retsina
It seems to me
That this fig is ripening in my hand

Gypsy traders come and go
With their leather goods
Tins of honey
And under the counter trade

Scored to a scratchy Rebetiko
Marika Ninou's ghost wailing
Love and death
Into the willing air

WINTER ON NISSIROS

And this too will pass into spring
With its almond blossom and Easter parades

The Square of Older People will fill
And coffee will be served with iced water
As talk for talk's sake
Lingers
Long past the meaning of the words

RETREAT

Days come and go

Waking, I stretch into loneliness

Out into the frost
The morning, thick with mist
Teems with concerns
Some important, some trivial
Most are lost
In the bleak landscape

Thorns, bare and gnarled
Cling to a few desiccated fruits
Red leathery allegories
The trees in the distance, bare and ethereal
Etched in an icy haze

A thicket in a barren field
Offers a different perspective
A robin foraging
The odour of leaf mould
White fungus fruiting on fallen wood
The renewal in decay
Gifts from kind ghosts

Brown earth

My breath on the air

I emerge into solitude

DISTRACTIONS

The day reveals itself
Distilled in birdsong
Dry mouthed and piss proud
It's time to get up
To find refuge
The bar on the corner
The clunk of cups, espresso
Human voices
The drone of a moped, a whiff of petrol
Night's remembrances
The pornography of pity
Camouflaged in the doing of day

FLICKER

I know what it is to need light.

A market town in January
The days forgetting themselves
Nights seem endless.

Walking with sin and regret
Absence howls a hungry song.

The shops long closed
Mock any possibilities
Their windows occluded
Present walls of darkness.

A plane tree hung with lights
Kindles something
A suggestion that life goes on.

WAKING ALONE

The day empties itself,
Its meaning lost before it begins,
Crowded out
In the dissonance of exile.

Enough is never enough,
Like it or not
You are your father's son,
Restless, hungry for more,
Sacrificing what is
For the next.

Age brings its opportunities
Nakedness and regrets,
As youth's fashions and conceits
Are discarded like spent matches
On a dancehall floor,
Peggy Lee having left the building.

Their iconography, like your history,
Scattered, vagrant, here and there,
Truths that await decoding:
The antithesis of those postcards you send
Fabricated for bragging rights
To impress the thinning shoals
Of wide eyed believers.

The truth lost to you
You cling to an amulet
Purchased as a joke
When you were young
And Avant-garde,
Sneering at superstition.

Turning its sorcery in your hand
You scan your forearm for an incantation,
The pigeon Latin
'Futuro est illiterate',
As fatuous
As the day it was tattooed,
Your course already set.

Yet despite this magic's anaemia
You gather yourself to face the crowd,
Another day full of piss and wind,
Its gear cut with baking soda,
You suck in your gut
And stride towards the wreckage.

N.W.5

Home 25 years on,
Meeting myself for a quiet drink,
I am as I was.
Whatever else has changed.

I map the sanctuary of my old haunt,
-The Bull and Gate-
With emergent eyes,
The fittings and faces have aged
But occupy the same space.
A virus of memory situates past and present.

I am yesterday in the corner,
A speck of the history
Without which this cannot exist.
The shadow of Christmas past
Who resents being a tourist on his own turf,
But things are as they are,
I want my dust to lodge in a crevice
On Kentish Town Road,
Where my dust belongs.

LOST AND FOUND

WINTER

This bare orchard
Stands as mute as religion,
Frost bitten and numb
Without sign of buds or blossom.

How I long for those bright banners,
With their promise of warm autumn evenings,
Eased with a lubricant of cider,
Tearing loose from tongues
Those moments that life is made of,
Wrapping the ambivalence of the hour,
As it does, in a cloak of celebration.

Here on the banks of the Suir,
These bleak sentries,
Magic trees of lore,
Offer no solace
From the river's dark anthem,
Its grey voice
Echoing a grim vocation,
Its turbulent course
Having given up
More men this year than salmon.

MASS IN SANTIAGO de COMPOSTELA

The processional hymn
rises from the ebbing Angelus bell

A nun sings
renewing her devotion
as a pitted stone cistern
is renewed by autumn rain

Her voice distilling
incense, ceremony and creed

A gift rooted
in the Camino's
power to transcend

ALL HALLOWS' EVE

This orchard
This sliver of land
Has no time for foolery
Things are as they are
And will move as they move
Regardless of concerns or conceit

The clocks have gone back
And the afternoon thickens with shadows
Omens of regret for the word too far
Promises made to pacify
Without thought for the consequences

Darkness offers some respite
As children with cold hands
Carry threats to the door of regret
The ghosts and ghouls of trick or treat
Driving out the demons within
Distractions from the sting of remembering
Those things that remain unatoned

FESTIVE

The day bleeds with sentimentality
Cardboard, dank sleeping bags, shivering dogs
Piled behind a hoarding
A windbreak if nothing else

Pools of water, the reflection of fairy lights
Fireflies drowning in piss
Holding off the reckoning
The Boxing Day sales start at 6am

LETTER TO ELLA

(On reading Ella's letter to Ken in the Normandy Invasion Museum)

Ella,
39 The Driveway,
Canvey Island,
Essex,
England.

Ella, forgive this intrusion,
But I read your letter today,
The one to your 'dark boy'.

They have placed it behind glass,
And there it defies,
A plowshare amongst swords,
Cutting to size,
The shabby ordnance of war.

Ella,
I hope your 'hubby' made it home,
And gave flesh to your love,
To spare you the howling pain,
Of reading of his warrior death,
In the passionless prose,
Of a telegraphic reply.

GRIEF, 1951. JACK B. YEATS

There is alchemy
in this painter's craft.

By infusing raw impasto
with a pulse of blood and bone,
He summons up a moment of grief
and the ache of the day that's in it.

AUTUMNAL MUSIC

As autumn composes
its first movements,
The old light their fires,
Thickening the air
with sweet plumes
of spiralling turf smoke.

On Main Street,
Mallow's citizenry bustle by
in a medley of allegretto steps
that thin into silence
as drizzle shimmers
gossamer on sullen street lamps
and a lone cello sobs
for all the darkness yet to come.

IN THOSE MOMENTS

His last breath
A bow across a cello
Then the silence

A deep muscular silence

Punctuated
By the redundant mechanics
Of pain control

IN A PROFESSIONAL CAPACITY

She handed me a piece of paper
Patterned with the cipher
Of a curiously rational hand

Night has become too dark
For me to swim to shore
My life belongs to history
My memory to you

And asked

"What was he thinking?
Was there anything I could have done?"

Mouthing platitudes,
Wishing I had more to offer her
I longed for his economy

EAVESDROPPING IN A CHIP SHOP

His disregard for her is structural,
Not the transitory disregard of the bad day
Or the hurt snipping of terrible news,
But the fruiting head
Of a lifetime of disregard,
Sneering and contemptuous,
Unleashed in the private parts of the day,
When he believes no audience is on hand
To hear his fawning, passive, coos,
Those choreographed kindnesses
For which she must feign delight,
Those moments of respite
She knows to be only public deep.

RATHMINES, 1936

Turning the holy pictures to the wall
He took a piece of bacon fat from his waistcoat pocket
Unwrapped it from a hanky and greased his 'old man'
Lubricant to sodomise his daughter
Her not being married
He didn't want her put in the family way
With all the shame that would bring on his name

OBJECT

Inside
grey justice
slowly turns
as a girl waits
heavy with duty
her body a pallbearer
to another

Outside huddled evangelists
make her a cause
brandishing images
of foetal destruction
urging this child
not to murder
another

They demand
what so many have before
a suitable offering
a fresh gore garland
from a green girl

TRANSFORMATION

Oscillating at the meeting
of surface and light
the chameleon lake
shimmers from slate blue to silver
etching its moment
on an atom of water and sky
that's driven hard and deep
into the lake's memory
on the prismal arc of a trout's back

THE ALCHEMY OF SNOW

Life can be lived tonight
as on no other

A portal of silence
to enter as part of
to be and not to observe
to become hunter and hunted
visceral
focused on breath, pulse and skin

A barn owl's silent flight
rabbit tracks in the snow
a moment of grace passes to memory
returns to stillness
as if it had never been

Yet is indelible

MOMENT

Three notes from a clarinet
Zephyrs above Playa Timmerou
Beach-side cafes glowing in the darkness

Made in the USA
Charleston, SC
26 March 2014